THE FIREBUGS

PLAYS BY MAX FRISCH
(Published by Hill and Wang)

THE CHINESE WALL

THE FIREBUGS

ANDORRA

MAX FRISCH: THREE PLAYS
    Don Juan, or The Love of Geometry
    The Great Rage of Philip Hotz
    When the War Was Over

BIOGRAPHY: A GAME

MAX FRISCH

THE FIREBUGS

(Herr Biedermann und die Brandstifter)

A Learning-Play Without a Lesson

Translated by
MORDECAI GORELIK

A Spotlight Dramabook
HILL AND WANG — NEW YORK

MAX FRISCH

Born in 1911 in Zurich (and thus old enough to have lived through two world wars), Max Frisch has been for some fifteen years one of the outstanding literary figures in Europe. That he has remained until recently almost totally unknown in America is partly a result of his own lack of interest in a world-wide reputation, but is probably more particularly a commentary on the present state of the theatre in America.

Frisch is—and has been throughout his adult life—an architect by profession, a writer by avocation, which may account for his persistent experimentalism and his indifference to commercial considerations.

Although Frisch had written several plays, novels, and stories before he wrote *The Chinese Wall*, it was this play that first brought him fame outside of Switzerland. It was followed by several other works exhibiting that peculiar bitter-sweet blend of ironic wit and profound despair that is the trademark of Frisch as a writer—*Graf Oederland* in 1951, *Don Juan, oder die Liebe zur Geometrie* in 1951, and *Herr Biedermann und die Brandstifter (The Firebugs)* in 1959. *Andorra*, a sensational success in Europe, was first produced in 1962.

The Firebugs is a good example of Frisch's indefatigable passion for revision. Originally written in 1951 as a radio play, it was reworked in 1953 into a stage play, and then in 1960 was re-revised and produced as *Biedermann und die Hölle*. The "Don Juan" of the play bearing his name first appeared as a minor character in *The Chinese Wall*. *Graf*

Oederland was originally an extended prose sketch in one of Frisch's published diaries.

In addition to his plays, Frisch has published several novels (two of which, *Stiller* and *Homo Faber*, have been translated into English), diaries, and various literary and political essays. He has in recent years received a number of literary prizes. He travels frequently; shortly after World War II, he spent a year in America on a Rockefeller grant.

Max Frisch is presently living near Zurich.

THE FIREBUGS

SCENE 1

CHARACTERS

GOTTLIEB BIEDERMANN
BABETTE, *his wife*
ANNA, *a maidservant*
SEPP SCHMITZ, *a wrestler*
WILLI EISENRING, *a waiter*
A POLICEMAN
A PH.D.
MRS. KNECHTLING
THE CHORUS OF FIREMEN

SCENE—A simultaneous setting, showing the living room and
        the attic of BIEDERMANN's house.
TIME—Now.

The stage is dark; then a match flares, illuminating the face of GOTTLIEB BIEDERMANN. *He is lighting a cigar, and as the stage grows more visible he looks about him. He is surrounded by firemen wearing their helmets.*

BIEDERMANN. You can't even light a cigar any more without thinking of houses on fire. . . . It's disgusting! [*He throws away the burning cigar and exits.*]

The firemen come forward in the manner of an antique CHORUS. *The town clock booms the quarter-hour.*

Chorus. Fellow citizens, we,
   Guardians of the city.
   Watchers, listeners,
   Friends of the friendly town.

Leader. Which pays our salaries.

Chorus. Uniformed, equipped,
   We guard your homes,
   Patrol your streets,
   Vigilant, tranquil.

Leader. Resting from time to time,
   But alert, unsleeping.

Chorus. Watching, listening,
   Lest hidden danger
   Come to light
   Too late.

3

The clock strikes half-hour.

Leader. Much goes up in flames,
    But not always
    Because of fate.

Chorus. Call it fate, they tell you,
    And ask no questions.
    But mischief alone
    Can destroy whole cities.

Leader. Stupidity alone——

Chorus. Stupidity, all-too-human——

Leader. Can undo our citizens,
    Our all-too-mortal citizens.

The clock strikes three-quarters.

Chorus. Use your head;
    A stitch in time saves nine.

Leader. Exactly.

Chorus. Just because it happened,
    Don't put the blame on God,
    Nor on our human nature,
    Nor on our fruitful earth,
    Nor on our radiant sun . . .
    Just because it happened,
    Must you call the damned thing Fate?

The clock strikes four-quarters.

Leader. Our watch begins.

The Chorus *sits. The clock strikes nine o'clock.*

SCENE 2

The Living Room. BIEDERMANN *is reading the paper and smoking a cigar.* ANNA, *the maidservant, in a white apron, brings him a bottle of wine.*

ANNA. Mr. Biedermann? [*No answer.*] Mr. Biedermann——

BIEDERMANN *puts down his paper.*

Biedermann. They ought to hang them! I've said so all along! Another fire! And always the same story: another peddler shoe-horning his way into somebody's attic—another "harmless" peddler—— [*He picks up the bottle.*] They ought to hang every one of them! [*He picks up the corkscrew.*]

Anna. He's still here, Mr. Biedermann. The peddler. He wants to talk to you.

Biedermann. I'm not in!

Anna. Yes, sir, I told him—an hour ago. He says he knows you. I can't throw him out, Mr. Biedermann.

Biedermann. Why not?

Anna. He's too strong.

Biedermann. Let him come to the office tomorrow.

Anna. Yes sir. I told him three times. He says he's not interested. He doesn't want any hair tonic.

Biedermann. What *does* he want?

Anna. Kindness, he says. Humanity.

Biedermann [*sniffs at the cork*]. Tell him I'll throw him out myself if he doesn't get going at once. [*He fills his glass*

7

carefully.] Humanity! [*He tastes the wine.*] Let him wait in the hall for me. If he's selling suspenders or razor blades . . . I'm not inhuman, you know, Anna. But they mustn't come into the house—I've told you that a hundred times! Even if we have three vacant beds, it's out of the question! Anybody knows what this sort of thing can lead to, these days——

ANNA *is about to go, when* SCHMITZ *enters. He is athletic, in a costume reminiscent partly of the prison, partly of the circus; his arms are tattooed and there are leather straps on his wrists.* ANNA *edges out.* BIEDERMANN *sips his wine, unaware of* SCHMITZ, *who waits until he turns around.*

Schmitz. Good evening. [BIEDERMANN *drops his cigar in surprise.*] Your cigar, Mr. Biedermann. [*He picks up the cigar and hands it to* BIEDERMANN.]

Biedermann. Look here——

Schmitz. Good evening.

Biedermann. What is this? I told the girl distinctly to have you wait in the hall.

Schmitz. My name is Schmitz.

Biedermann. Without even knocking!

Schmitz. Sepp Schmitz. [*Silence.*] Good evening.

Biedermann. What do you want?

Schmitz. You needn't worry, Mr. Biedermann. I'm not a peddler.

Biedermann. No?

Schmitz. I'm a wrestler. I mean I *used* to be.

Biedermann. And now?

Schmitz. Unemployed. [*Pause.*] Don't worry, sir, I'm not looking for a job—I'm fed up with wrestling. I came in here because it's raining hard outside. [*Pause.*] It's warm in here. [*Pause.*] I hope I'm not intruding . . . [*Pause.*]

Biedermann. Cigar? [*He offers one.*]

Schmitz. You know, it's awful, Mr. Biedermann—with a build like mine, everybody gets scared. . . . Thank you. [BIEDERMANN *gives him a light.*] Thank you. [*They stand there, smoking.*]

Biedermann. Get to the point.

Schmitz. My name is Schmitz.

Biedermann. You've said that . . . Delighted.

Schmitz. I have no place to sleep. [*He holds the cigar to his nose, enjoying the aroma.*] No place to sleep.

Biedermann. Would you like—some bread?

Schmitz. If that's all there is.

Biedermann. A glass of wine?

Schmitz. Bread and wine . . . If it's no trouble, sir; if it's no trouble. [BIEDERMANN *goes to the door.*]

Biedermann. Anna! [*He comes back.*]

Schmitz. The girl said you were going to throw me out personally, Mr. Biedermann, but I knew you didn't mean it. [ANNA *has entered.*]

Biedermann. Anna, bring another glass.

Anna. Yes sir.

Biedermann. And some bread.

Schmitz. And if you don't mind, miss, a little butter. Some cheese or cold cuts. Only don't go to any trouble. Some pickles, a tomato or something, some mustard—whatever you have, miss.

Anna. Yes sir.

Schmitz. If it's no trouble.

ANNA *exits.*

Biedermann. You told the girl you know me.

Schmitz. That's right, sir.

Biedermann. How do you know me?

Schmitz. I know you at your best, sir. Last night at the pub—you didn't see me; I was sitting in the corner. The whole place liked the way you kept banging the table.

Biedermann. What did I say?

Schmitz. Exactly the right thing, Mr. Biedermann! [*He takes a puff at his cigar.*] "They ought to hang them all! The sooner the better—the whole bunch! All those firebugs!"

BIEDERMANN *offers him a chair.*

Biedermann. Sit down. [SCHMITZ *sits.*]

Schmitz. This country needs men like you, sir.

Biedermann. I know, but——

Schmitz. No buts, Mr. Biedermann, no buts. You're the old-time type of solid citizen. That's why your slant on things——

Biedermann. Certainly, but——

Schmitz. That's why.

Biedermann. Why what?

Schmitz. You have a conscience. Everybody in the pub could see that. A solid conscience.

Biedermann. Naturally, but——

Schmitz. Mr. Biedermann, it's not natural at all. Not these days. In the circus, where I did my wrestling, for instance—before it burned down, the whole damned circus—our manager, for instance; you know what he told me? "Sepp," he says, "You know me. They can shove it. What do I need a conscience for?" Just like that! "What my animals need is a whip," he says. That's the sort of guy he is! "A conscience!" [*He sneers.*] "If anybody has a conscience, you can bet it's a bad one." [*Enjoying his cigar.*] God rest him!

Biedermann. Is he dead?

Schmitz. Burned to a cinder, with everything he owned. [*A pendulum clock strikes nine.*]

Biedermann. I don't know what's keeping that girl so long.

Schmitz. I've got time. [*Their eyes meet.*] You haven't an empty bed in the house, Mr. Biedermann. The girl told me.

Biedermann. Why do you laugh?

Schmitz. "Sorry, no empty bed." That's what they all say. . . . What's the result? Somebody like me, with no place to sleep—— Anyway I don't want a bed.

Biedermann. No?

Schmitz. Oh, I'm used to sleeping on the floor. My father was a miner. I'm used to it. [*He puffs at his cigar.*] No apologies necessary, sir. You're not one of those birds who sounds off in public—when *you* say something I believe it. What are things coming to if people can't believe each other any more? Nothing but suspicion all over! Am I right? But *you* still believe in yourself and others. Right? You're about the only man left in this town who doesn't say right off that people like us are firebugs.

Biedermann. Here's an ash tray.

Schmitz. Or am I wrong? [*He taps the ash off his cigar carefully.*] People don't believe in God any more—they believe in the Fire Department.

Biedermann. What do you mean by that?

Schmitz. Nothing but the truth.

ANNA comes in with a tray.

Anna. We have no cold cuts.

Schmitz. This will do, miss, this will do fine. Only you forgot the mustard.

Anna. Excuse me.   [*Exits.*

Biedermann. Eat. [*He fills the glasses.*]

Schmitz. You don't get a reception like this every place you go, Mr. Biedermann, let me tell you! I've had some experiences! Somebody like me comes to the door—no necktie, no place to stay, hungry; "Sit down," they say, "have a seat"—and meanwhile they call the police. How do you like that? All I ask for is a place to sleep, that's all. A good wrestler who's wrestled all his life—and some bird who never wrestled at all grabs me by the collar! "What's this?" I ask myself. I turn around just to look, and first thing you know he's broken his shoulder! [*Picks up his glass.*] *Prosit!* [*They drink, and* Schmitz *starts eating.*]

Biedermann. That's how it goes, these days. You can't open a newspaper without reading about another arson case. The same old story: another peddler asking for a place to sleep, and next morning the house is in flames. I mean to say . . . well, frankly, I can understand a certain amount of distrust . . . [*Reaches for his newspaper.*] Look at this! [*He lays the paper next to* Schmitz's *plate.*]

Schmitz. I saw it.

Biedermann. A whole district in flames. [*He gets up to show it to* Schmitz.] Just read that! [Schmitz *eats, reads, and drinks.*]

Schmitz. Is this wine Beaujolais?

Biedermann. Yes.

Schmitz. Could be a little warmer. [*He reads, over his plate.*] "Apparently the fire was planned and executed in the same way as the previous one." [*They exchange a glance.*]

Biedermann. Isn't that the limit?

Schmitz. That's why I don't care to read newspapers. Always the same thing.

Biedermann. Yes, yes, naturally . . . But that's no answer to the problem, to stop reading the papers. After all, you have to know what you're up against.

Schmitz. What for?

Biedermann. Why, because.

Schmitz. It'll happen anyway, Mr. Biedermann, it'll happen anyway. [*He sniffs the sausage.*] God's will. [*He slices the sausage.*]

Biedermann. You think so?

ANNA *brings the mustard.*

Schmitz. Thank you, miss, thank you.

Anna. Anything else you'd like?

Schmitz. Not today. [ANNA *stops at the door.*] Mustard is my favorite dish. [*He squeezes mustard out of the tube.*]

Biedermann. How do you mean, God's will?

Schmitz. God knows . . . [*He continues to eat with his eye on the paper.*] "Expert opinion is that apparently the fire was planned and executed in the same way as the previous one." [*He laughs shortly, and fills his glass.*]

Anna. Mr. Biedermann?

Biedermann. What is it now?

Anna. Mr. Knechtling would like to speak to you.

Biedermann. Knechtling? Now? Knechtling?

Anna. He says—— .

Biedermann. Out of the question.

Anna. He says he simply can't understand you.

Biedermann. Why must he understand me?

Anna. He has a sick wife and three children, he says——

Biedermann. Out of the question! [*He gets up impatiently.*] Mr. Knechtling! Mr. Knechtling! Let Mr. Knechtling leave me alone, dammit! Or let him get a lawyer! Please—let him! I'm through for the day. . . . Mr. Knechtling! All this to-do because I gave him his notice! Let him get a lawyer, by all means! I'll get one, too. . . . Royalties on his invention! Let him stick his head in the gas stove or get a lawyer! If Mr. Knechtling can afford indulging in lawyers! Please—let him! [*Controlling himself, with a glance at* SCHMITZ.] Tell Mr. Knechtling I have a visitor. [ANNA *exits.*] Excuse me.

Schmitz. This is your house, Mr. Biedermann.

Biedermann. How is the food? [*He sits, observing* SCHMITZ, *who attacks his food with enthusiasm.*]

Schmitz. Who'd have thought you could still find it, these days?

Biedermann. Mustard?

Schmitz. Humanity! [*He screws the top of the mustard tube back on.*] Here's what I mean: you don't grab me by the collar and throw me out in the rain, Mr. Biedermann. *That's* what we need, Mr. Biedermann! Humanity! [*He pours himself a drink.*] God will reward you! [*He drinks with gusto.*]

Biedermann. You mustn't think I'm inhuman, Mr. Schmitz.

Schmitz. Mr. Biedermann!

Biedermann. That's what Mrs. Knechtling thinks.

Schmitz. Would you be giving me a place to sleep tonight if you were inhuman?—Ridiculous!

Biedermann. Of course!

Schmitz. Even if it's a bed in the attic. [*He puts down his glass.*] Now our wine's the right temperature. [*The doorbell rings.*] Police?

Biedermann. My wife. [*The doorbell rings again.*] Come along, Mr. Schmitz. . . . But mind you, no noise! My wife has a heart condition——

Women's voices are heard offstage. BIEDERMANN *motions to* SCHMITZ *to hurry. They pick up the tray, bottles, and glasses and tiptoe toward stage right, where the* CHORUS *is sitting.*

Biedermann. Excuse me! [*He steps over the bench.*]

Schmitz. Excuse me! [*He steps over the bench. He and* BIEDERMANN *disappear.*]

BABETTE BIEDERMANN *enters, left, accompanied by* ANNA, *who takes her packages.*

Babette. Where's my husband?—You know, Anna, we're not narrow-minded, and I don't mind your having a boy friend. But if you're going to park him in the house——

Anna. But I don't have a boy friend, Mrs. Biedermann.

Babette. Then whose rusty bicycle is that, outside the front door? It scared me to death!

The Attic. BIEDERMANN *switches on the light and gestures for* SCHMITZ *to come in. They speak in whispers.*

Biedermann. Here's the light switch. If you get cold, there's an old sheepskin around here somewhere. Only for heaven's sake be quiet! Take off your shoes! [SCHMITZ *puts down the tray, takes off one shoe.*] Mr. Schmitz?

Schmitz. Mr. Biedermann?

Biedermann. You promise me, though, you're not a firebug? [SCHMITZ *starts to laugh.*] Sh!! [*He nods good night and exits, closing the door.* SCHMITZ *takes off his other shoe.*]

The Living Room. BABETTE *has heard something; she listens, frightened. Then, relieved, she turns to the audience.*

Babette. Gottlieb, my husband, promised to go up to the attic every evening, personally, to see if there is any firebug up there. I'm so thankful! Otherwise I'd lie awake half the night.   [BABETTE *exits.*

The Attic. SCHMITZ, *now in his socks, goes to the light switch and snaps out the light.*

Below.

Chorus. Fellow citizens, we,
   Shield of the innocent,
   Guardians ever-tranquil,
   Shield of the sleeping city.
   Standing or
   Sitting,
   Ever on guard.

Leader. Taking a quiet smoke, now and again, to pass the time.

Chorus. Watching,
   Listening,
   Lest malignant fire leap out
   Above these cozy rooftops
   To undo our city.

The town clock strikes three.

Leader. Everyone knows we're here,
   Ready on call. [*He fills his pipe.*]

Chorus. Who turns the light on at this wee, small hour?
Woe!

Nerve-shattered,
Uncomforted by sleep,
The wife appears.

BABETTE *enters in a bathrobe.*

Babette. Somebody coughed! [*A snore.*] Gottlieb, did you
hear that? [*A cough.*] Somebody's there! [*A snore.*] That's
men for you! A sleeping pill is all they need!

The town clock strikes four.

Leader. Four o'clock. [BABETTE *turns off the light again.*]
We were not called. [*He puts away his pipe. The stage
lightens.*]

Chorus. O radiant sun!
O godlike eye!
Light up the day above our cozy roofs!
Thanks be!
No harm has come to our sleeping town.
Not yet.
Thanks be! [*The* CHORUS *sits.*]

SCENE 3

The Living Room. BIEDERMANN, *his hat and coat on, his brief case under his arm, is drinking a cup of coffee standing up, and is speaking to* BABETTE, *who is offstage.*

BIEDERMANN. For the last time—he's not a firebug!

Babette's Voice. How do you know?

Biedermann. I asked him myself, point blank—— Can't you think of anything else in this world, Babette? You and your firebugs—you're enough to drive a man insane!

BABETTE *enters with the cream pitcher.*

Babette. Don't yell at me.

Biedermann. I'm not yelling at you, Babette, I'm merely yelling. [*She pours cream into his cup.*] I have to go. [*He drinks his coffee. It's too hot.*] If everybody goes around thinking everybody else is an arsonist—— You've got to have a little trust in people, Babette, just a little! [*He looks at his watch.*]

Babette. I don't agree. You're too good-hearted, Gottlieb. You listen to the promptings of your heart, but I'm the one who can't sleep all night. : . . I'll give him some breakfast and then I'll send him on his way, Gottlieb.

Biedermann. Do that.

Babette. In a nice way, of course, without offending him.

Biedermann. Do that. [*He puts his cup down.*] I have to see my lawyer. [*He gives* BABETTE *a perfunctory kiss. They do not notice* SCHMITZ, *who enters, the sheepskin around his shoulders.*]

21

Babette. Why did you give Knechtling his notice?

Biedermann. I don't need him any more.

Babette. But you were always so pleased with him!

Biedermann. That's just what he's presuming on, now! Royalties on his invention—that's what he wants! Invention! Our Hormotone hair tonic is merchandise, that's all—it's no invention! All those good folk who pour our tonic on their domes could use their own piss for all the good it does them!

Babette. Gottlieb!

Biedermann. It's true, though. [*He checks to see if he has everything in his brief case.*] I'm too good-hearted—you're right. But I'll take care of this Knechtling! [*He is about to go when he sees* SCHMITZ.]

Schmitz. Good morning, everybody.

Biedermann. Mr. Schmitz—[SCHMITZ *offers his hand.*]

Schmitz. Call me Sepp.

Biedermann [*ignores his hand*]. My wife will speak with you, Mr. Schmitz. I have to go, I'm sorry. Good luck. . . . [*Changes his mind and shakes hands.*] Good luck, Sepp.
                                        [BIEDERMANN *exits.*

Schmitz. Good luck, Gottlieb. [BABETTE *looks at him.*] That's your husband's name, isn't it—Gottlieb?

Babette. How did you sleep?

Schmitz. Thank you, madam—kind of freezing. But I made use of this sheepskin. Reminded me of old days in the mines. I'm used to the cold.

Babette. Your breakfast is ready.

Schmitz. Really, madam! [*She motions for him to sit.*] No, really, I—— [*She fills his cup.*]

Babette. You must pitch in, Sepp. You have a long way to go, I'm sure.

Sepp. How do you mean? [*She points to the chair again.*]

Babette. Would you care for a soft-boiled egg?

Schmitz. Two.

Babette. Anna!

Schmitz. I feel right at home, madam. [*He sits.*]

ANNA enters.

Babette. Two soft-boiled eggs.

Anna. Yes, ma'am.

Schmitz. Three and a half minutes.

ANNA starts to leave.

Schmitz. Miss—— [ANNA *stops at the door.*] Good morning.

Anna. Morning.   [*She exits.*

Schmitz. The look she gave me! If it was up to her I'd still be out there in the pouring rain. [BABETTE *fills his cup.*]

Babette. Mr. Schmitz——

Schmitz. Yeah?

Babette. If I may speak frankly——

Schmitz. Your hands are shaking, madam.

Babette. Mr. Schmitz——

Schmitz. What's troubling you?

Babette. Here's some cheese.

Schmitz. Thank you.

Babette. Marmalade.

Schmitz. Thank you.

Babette. Honey.

Schmitz. One at a time, madam, one at a time. [*He leans back, eating his bread and butter; attentively.*] Well?

Babette. Frankly, Mr. Schmitz——

Schmitz. Just call me Sepp.

Babette. Frankly——

Schmitz. You'd like to get rid of me.

Babette. No, Mr. Schmitz, no! I wouldn't put it that way——

Schmitz. How would you put it? [*He takes some cheese.*] Tilsit cheese is my dish. [*He leans back, eating; attentively.*] Madam thinks I'm a firebug.

Babette. Please don't misunderstand me. What did I say? The last thing I want to do is hurt your feelings, Mr. Schmitz. . . . You've got me all confused now. Who ever mentioned firebugs? Even your manners, Mr. Schmitz; I'm not complaining.

Schmitz. I know. I have no manners.

Babette. That's not it, Mr. Schmitz——

Schmitz. I smack my lips when I eat.

Babette. Nonsense.

Schmitz. That's what they used to tell me at the orphanage: "Schmitz, don't smack your lips when you eat!" [BA-BETTE *is about to pour more coffee.*]

Babette. You don't understand me. Really, you don't in the least! [SCHMITZ *places his hand over his cup.*]

Schmitz. I'm going.

Babette. Mr. Schmitz.

Schmitz. I'm going.

Babette. Another cup of coffee? [*He shakes his head.*] Half a cup? [*He shakes his head.*] You mustn't take it like that, Mr. Schmitz. I didn't mean to hurt your feelings. I didn't say a single word about you making noises while you eat. [*He gets up.*] Have I hurt your feelings? [*He folds his napkin.*]

Schmitz. It's not your lookout, madam, if I have no manners. My father was a coal miner. Where would people like us get any manners? Starving and freezing, madam—that's something I don't mind; but no education, madam, no manners, madam, no refinement——

Babette. I understand.

Schmitz. I'm going.

Babette. Where?

Schmitz. Out in the rain.

Babette. Oh, no!

Schmitz. I'm used to it.

Babette. Mr. Schmitz . . . don't look at me like that. Your father was a miner—I can understand it. You had an unfortunate childhood——

Schmitz. No childhood at all, madam. [*He looks down at his fingers.*] None at all. My mother died when I was seven. . . . [*He turns away to wipe his eyes.*]

Babette. Sepp!— But Sepp——

ANNA *brings the soft-boiled eggs.*

Anna. Anything else you'd like? [*She gets no answer; exits.*]

Babette. I haven't ordered you to leave, Mr. Schmitz. I never said that. After all, what did I say? You misunderstand me, Mr. Schmitz. Really, I mean it—won't you believe me? [*She takes his sleeve—with some hesitation.*] Come, Sepp— finish eating! [SCHMITZ *sits down again.*] What do you take us for? I haven't even noticed that you smack your lips. Honestly! Even if I did—we don't care a bit about external things. We're not like that at all, Mr. Schmitz. . . . [*He cracks his egg.*]

Schmitz. God will reward you!

Babette. Here's the salt. [*He eats the egg with a spoon.*]

Schmitz. It's true, madam, you didn't order me away. You didn't say a word about it. That's true. Pardon me, madam, for not understanding.

Babette. Is the egg all right?

Schmitz. A little soft . . . Do pardon me, won't you? [*He has finished the egg.*] What were you going to say, madam, when you started to say, very frankly——

Babette. Well, I was going to say . . . [*He cracks the second egg.*]

Schmitz. God will reward you. [*He starts on the second egg.*] My friend Willi says you can't find it any more, he says. Private charity. No fine people left; everything State-controlled. No real people left, these days . . . he says. The world is going to the dogs—that's why! [*He salts his egg.*] Wouldn't he be surprised to get a breakfast like this! Wouldn't he open his eyes, my friend, Willi! [*The doorbell rings.*] That could be him. [*It rings again.*]

Babette. Who is Willi?

Schmitz. You'll see, madam. Willi's refined. Used to be a waiter at the Metropol. Before it burned down . . .

Babette. Burned down?

Schmitz. Headwaiter.

ANNA *enters.*

Babette. Who is it?

Anna. A gentleman.

Babette. What does he want?

Anna. From the fire insurance, he says. To look over the house. [BABETTE *gets up.*] He's wearing a frock coat——

Schmitz. My friend Willi!

Chorus. Now two of them dismay us——
    Two bicycles, both rusty.
    To whom do they belong?

Leader. One yesterday's arrival.
    One today's.

Chorus. Woe!

Leader. Night once again, and our watch.

The town clock strikes.

Chorus. How much the coward fears where nothing threat-
    ens!
    Dreading his own shadow,
    Whirling at each sound,
    Until his fears overtake him
    At his own bedside!

The town clock strikes.

Leader. They never leave their room, these two.
    What is the reason?

The town clock strikes.

Chorus. Blind, ah, blind is the weakling!
    Trembling, expectant of evil,
    Yet hoping somehow to avoid it!
    Defenseless!
    Ah, weary of menacing evil,
    With open arms he receives it!

The town clock strikes.

Woe! [*The* CHORUS *sits.*]

SCENE 4

The Attic. SCHMITZ *is dressed as before.* EISENRING *has removed the jacket of his frock coat and is in a white vest and shirt sleeves. He and* SCHMITZ *are rolling tin barrels into a corner of the attic. The barrels are the type used for storing gasoline. Both vagabonds are in their socks and are working as quietly as they can.*

EISENRING. Quiet! Quiet!

Schmitz. Suppose he calls the police?

Eisenring. Keep going.

Schmitz. What then?

Eisenring. Easy! Easy!

They roll the barrels up to those already stacked in the shadows. EISENRING *wipes his fingers with some cotton waste.*

Eisenring. Why would he call the police?

Schmitz. Why not?

Eisenring. Because he's guilty himself—that's why. [*He throws away the rag.*] Above a certain income every citizen is guilty one way or another. Have no fear. [*Doves are heard cooing.*] It's morning. Bedtime! [*There is a sudden knocking on the locked door.*]

Biedermann's Voice. Open up! Open up, there! [*He pounds on the door and shakes it.*]

Eisenring. That's no call for breakfast.

Biedermann's Voice. Open, I say! Immediately!

Schmitz. He was never like that before.

31

The banging on the door gets louder. Without haste, but briskly, EISENRING puts on his jacket, straightens his tie and flicks the dust from his trousers. Then he opens the door. BIEDERMANN enters. He is in his bathrobe. He does not see EISENRING, who is now behind the open door.

Biedermann. Mr. Schmitz!

Schmitz. Good morning, sir. I hope this noise didn't wake you.

Biedermann. Mr. Schmitz——

Schmitz. It won't happen again, I assure you.

Biedermann. Leave this house! [*Pause.*] I say leave this house!

Schmitz. When?

Biedermann. At once!

Schmitz. But——

Biedermann. Or my wife will call the police. And I can't and won't stop her.

Schmitz. Hm . . .

Biedermann. I said right away, and I mean it. What are you waiting for? [SCHMITZ *picks up his shoes.*] I'll have no discussion about it!

Schmitz. Did I say anything?

Biedermann. If you think you can do as you like here because you're a wrestler—— A racket like that, all night—— [*Points to the door.*] Out, I say! Get out! [SCHMITZ *turns to* EISENRING.]

Schmitz. He was never like that before. . . . [BIEDERMANN *sees* EISENRING *and is speechless.*]

Eisenring. My name is Eisenring.

Biedermann. What's the meaning of this?

Eisenring. Willi Maria Eisenring.

Biedermann. Why are there two of you suddenly? [SCHMITZ *and* EISENRING *look at each other.*] Without even asking!

Eisenring. There, you see!

Biedermann. What's going on here?

Eisenring [*to* SCHMITZ]. Didn't I tell you? Didn't I say it's no way to act, Sepp? Where are your manners? Without even asking! Suddenly two of us!

Biedermann. I'm beside myself!

Eisenring. There, you see! [*He turns to* BIEDERMANN.] That's what I told him! [*Back to* SCHMITZ.] Didn't I?

SCHMITZ hangs his head.

Biedermann. Where do you think you are? Let's get one thing clear, gentlemen—I'm the owner of this house! I ask you—where do you think you are? [*Pause.*]

Eisenring. Answer when the gentleman asks you something! [*Pause.*]

Schmitz. Willi is a friend of mine. . . .

Biedermann. And so?

Schmitz. We were schoolmates together.

Biedermann. And so?

Schmitz. And so I thought . . .

Biedermann. What?

Schmitz. I thought . . . [*Pause.*]

Eisenring. You didn't think! [*He turns to* BIEDERMANN.] I understand fully, Mr. Biedermann. All you want to do is what's right—let's get that clear! [*He shouts at* SCHMITZ.] You think the owner of this house is going to be pushed around? [*He turns to* BIEDERMANN *again.*] Sepp didn't consult you at all?

Biedermann. Not a word!

Eisenring. Sepp——

Biedermann. Not one word!

Eisenring [*to* SCHMITZ]. And then you're surprised when people throw you out in the street! [*He laughs contemptuously.*]

Biedermann. There's nothing to laugh at, gentlemen! I'm serious! My wife has a heart condition——

Eisenring. There, you see!

Biedermann. She didn't sleep half the night because of your noise. And anyway, what are you doing here? [*He looks around.*] What the devil are these barrels doing here? [SCHMITZ *and* EISENRING *look hard where there are no barrels.*] If you don't mind—what are these? [*He raps on a barrel.*]

Schmitz. Barrels . . .

Biedermann. Where did *they* come from?

Schmitz. Do you know, Willi? Where they came from?

Eisenring. It says "Imported" on the label.

Biedermann. Gentlemen——

Eisenring. It says so on them somewhere! [EISENRING *and* SCHMITZ *look for a label.*]

Biedermann. I'm speechless! What do you think you're doing? My whole attic is full of barrels—floor to ceiling! All the way from floor to ceiling!

Eisenring. I knew it! [EISENRING *swings around.*] Sepp had it figured out all wrong. [*To* SCHMITZ.] Six by eight meters, you said. There's not twenty square meters in this attic!— I couldn't leave my barrels in the street, Mr. Biedermann; you can understand that——

Biedermann. I don't understand a thing! [SCHMITZ *shows him a label.*]

Schmitz. Here, Mr. Biedermann—here's the label.

Biedermann. I'm speechless.

Schmitz. Here it says where they come from. Here.

Biedermann. Simply speechless. [*He inspects the label.*]

The Living Room. ANNA *leads a* POLICEMAN *in.*

Anna. I'll call him. What's it about, officer?

Policeman. Official business. [ANNA *exits. The* POLICEMAN *waits.*]

The Attic.

Biedermann. Is it true? Is it true?

Eisenring. Is what true?

Biedermann. What's printed on this label? [*He shows them the label.*] What do you take me for? I've never in my life seen anything like this! Do you think I can't read? [*They look at the label.*] Just look! [*He laughs sarcastically.*] Gasoline! [*In the voice of a district attorney.*] What is in those barrels?

Eisenring. Gasoline!

Biedermann. Never mind your jokes! I'm asking you for the last time—what's in those barrels? You know as well as I do—attics are no place for gasoline! [*He runs his finger over one of the barrels.*] If you don't mind—just smell that for yourselves! [*He waves his finger under their noses.*] Is that gasoline or isn't it? [*They sniff and exchange glances.*]

Eisenring. It is.

Schmitz. It is.

Both. No doubt whatever.

Biedermann. Are you insane? My whole attic full of gasoline——

Schmitz. That's just why we don't smoke up here, Mr. Biedermann.

Biedermann. What do you think you're doing? A thing like that—when every single newspaper is warning people to watch out for fires! My wife will have a heart attack!

Eisenring. There, you see!

Biedermann. Don't keep saying, "There, you see!"

Eisenring. You can't do that to a lady, Sepp. Not to a housewife. I know housewives. [ANNA *calls up the stairs.*]

Anna. Mr. Biedermann! Mr. Biedermann! [BIEDERMANN *shuts the door.*]

Biedermann. Mr. Schmitz! Mr.——

Eisenring. Eisenring.

Biedermann. If you don't get these barrels out of the house this instant—and I mean this instant——

Eisenring. You'll call the police.

Biedermann. Yes!

Schmitz. There, you see! [ANNA *calls up the stairs.*]

Anna. Mr. Biedermann!

Biedermann [*lowers his voice*]. That's my last word.

Eisenring. Which word?

Biedermann. I won't stand for it! I won't stand for gasoline in my attic! Once and for all! [*There is a knock at the door.*] I'm coming! [*He opens the door.*]

The POLICEMAN *enters.*

Policeman. Ah, there you are, Mr. Biedermann! You don't have to come down; I won't take much of your time.

Biedermann. Good morning!

Policeman. Good morning!

Eisenring. Morning!

Schmitz. Morning!

> SCHMITZ *and* EISENRING *nod courteously.*

Policeman. There's been an accident.

Biedermann. Good Heavens!

Policeman. An elderly man. His wife says he used to work for you. . . . An inventor. Put his head inside his kitchen stove last night. [*He consults his notebook.*] Knechtling, Johann. Number 11 Ross Street. [*He puts his notebook away.*] Did you know anybody by that name?

Biedermann. I——

Policeman. Maybe you'd rather we talked about this privately, Mr. Biedermann?

Biedermann. Yes.

Policeman. It doesn't concern these employees of yours.

Biedermann. No . . . [*He stops at the door.*] If anyone wants me, gentlemen, I'll be at the police station. I'll be right back.

> SCHMITZ *and* EISENRING *nod.*

Policeman. Mr. Biedermann——

Biedermann. Let's go.

Policeman. What have you got in those barrels?

Biedermann. These?

Policeman. If I may ask?

Biedermann. . . . Hair tonic . . . [*He looks at* SCHMITZ *and* EISENRING.]

Eisenring. Hormotone. Science's gift to the well-groomed.

Schmitz. Try a bottle today.

Eisenring. You won't regret it.

Both. Hormotone. Hormotone. Hormotone. [*The* POLICE-MAN *laughs.*]

Biedermann. Is he dead? [*He and the* POLICEMAN *exit.*]

Eisenring. A real sweetheart!

Schmitz. Didn't I tell you?

Eisenring. But he didn't mention breakfast.

Schmitz. He was never like that before. . . .

Eisenring [*reaching in his pocket*]. Have you got the detonator?

Schmitz [*feeling in his pocket*]. He was never like that before.

Downstairs.

Chorus. O radiant sun!
    O godlike eye!
    Light up the day again above our cozy roofs!

Leader. Today same as yesterday.

Chorus. Hail!

Leader. No harm has come to our sleeping city.

Chorus. Hail!

Leader. Not yet . . .

Chorus. Hail!

Traffic noises offstage; honking, streetcars.

Leader. Wise is man,
    And able to ward off most perils,
    If, sharp of mind and alert,
    He heeds signs of coming disaster
    In time.

Chorus. And if he does not?

Leader. He, who
    Attentive to possible dangers,
    Studies his newspaper daily—
    Is daily, at breakfast, dismayed
    By distant tidings, whose meaning
    Is daily digested to spare him
    Fatigue of his own muddled brain work—
    Learning daily what's happened, afar—
    Can he so quickly discern
    What is happening under his roof?
    Things that are——

Chorus. Unpublished!

Leader. Disgraceful!

Chorus. Inglorious!

Leader. Real!

Chorus. Things not easy to face!
    For, if he——

        The LEADER *interrupts with a gesture.*

Leader. He's coming.

        The CHORUS *breaks formation.*

Chorus. No harm has come to the sleeping city.
    No harm yesterday or today.
    Ignoring all omens,
    The freshly shaven citizen
    Speeds to his office. . . .

Enter BIEDERMANN *in hat and coat, his brief case under his
arm.*

Biedermann. Taxi! . . . Taxi! . . . Taxi! [*The* CHORUS
is in his way.] What's the trouble?

Chorus. Woe!

Biedermann. What's up?

Chorus. Woe!

Biedermann. You've said already!

Chorus. Three times woe!

Biedermann. But why?

Leader. All-too-strangely a fiery prospect
    Unfolds to our eyes.
    And to yours.
    Shall I be plainer?
    Gasoline in your attic——

Biedermann [*shouts*]. Is that *your* business? [*Silence.*] Let me through—I have to see my lawyer—— What do you want of me? I'm not guilty. . . . [*Unnerved.*] What's this— an inquisition? [*Masterfully.*] Let me through, please!

The C<small>HORUS</small> remains motionless.

Chorus. Far be it from us, the Chorus,
    To judge a hero of drama——

Leader. But we *do* see the oncoming peril,
    See clearly the menacing danger!

Chorus. Making a simple inquiry
    About an impending disaster—
    Uttering, merely, a warning—
    Civic-minded, the Chorus comes forward,
    Bathed, alas, in cold sweat,
    In half-fainting fear of that moment
    That calls for the hoses of firemen!

B<small>IEDERMANN</small> looks at his wrist watch.

Biedermann. I'm in a hurry.

Chorus. Woe!

Leader. All that gasoline, Gottlieb
    Biedermann!
    How could you take it?

Biedermann. Take it?

Leader. You know very well,
   The world is a brand for the burning!
   Yet, knowing it, what did you think?

Biedermann. Think? [*He appraises the* CHORUS.] My dear sirs, I am a free and independent citizen. I can think anything I like. What are all these questions? I have the right, my dear sirs, not to think at all if I feel like it! Aside from the fact that whatever goes on under my own roof—— Let's get one thing clear, gentlemen: I am the owner of the house!

Chorus. Sacred, sacred to us
   Is property,
   Whatever befall!
   Though we be scorched,
   Though we be cindered—
   Sacred, sacred to us!

Biedermann. Well, then—— [*Silence.*] Why can't I go through? [*Silence.*] Why must you always imagine the worst? Where will that get you? All I want is some peace and quiet, not a thing more. . . . As for those two gentlemen—aside from the fact that I have other troubles right now . . . [BABETTE *enters in street clothes.*] What do *you* want here?

Babette. Am I interrupting?

Biedermann. Can't you see I'm in conference? [BABETTE *nods to the* CHORUS, *then whispers in* BIEDERMANN's *ear.*] With ribbons, of course. Never mind the cost. As long as it's a wreath. [BABETTE *nods to the* CHORUS.]

Babette. Excuse me, sirs.   [*She exits.*

Biedermann. To cut it short, gentlemen, I'm fed up! You and your firebugs! I don't even go to the pub any more— that's how fed up I am! Is there nothing else to talk about these days? Let's get one thing straight—if you go around thinking everybody except yourself is an arsonist, how are things ever going to improve? A little trust in people, for heaven's sake! A little good will! Why keep looking at the bad side? Why go on the assumption that everybody else is a firebug? A little confidence, a little—— [*Pause.*] You can't go on living in fear! [*Pause.*] You think I closed my eyes last night for one instant? I'm not an imbecile, you know! Gasoline is gasoline! I had the worst kind of thoughts running through my head last night. . . . I climbed up on the table to listen—even got up on the bureau and put my ear to the ceiling! They were snoring, mind you—snoring! At least four times I climbed up on that bureau. Peacefully snoring! Just the same I got as far as the stairs, once—believe it or not—in my pajamas—and frantic, I tell you—frantic! I was all ready to wake up those two scoundrels and throw them out in the street, along with their barrels. Single-handedly, without compunction, in the middle of the night!

Chorus. Single-handedly?

Biedermann. Yes.

Chorus. Without compunction?

Biedermann. Yes.

Chorus. In the middle of the night?

Biedermann. Just about to! If my wife hadn't come after me, afraid I'd catch cold—— [*Embarrassed, he reaches for a cigar.*]

Leader. How shall I put it?
　　Sleepless he passed the night.
　　That they'd take advantage of a man's good nature—
　　Was that conceivable?
　　Suspicion came over him. Why?

BIEDERMANN *lights his cigar.*

Chorus. No, it's not easy for the citizen,
　　Tough in business

But really soft of heart,
Always ready,
Ready always to do good.

Leader. If that's how he happens to feel.

Chorus. Hoping that goodness
Will come of goodness.
How mistaken can you be?

Biedermann. What are you getting at?

Chorus. It seems to us there's a stink of gasoline.

BIEDERMANN *sniffs.*

Biedermann. I don't smell anything.

Chorus. Woe to us!

Biedermann. Not a thing.

Chorus. Woe to us!

Leader. How soon he's got accustomed to bad smells!

Chorus. Woe to us!

Biedermann. And don't keep giving us that defeatism, gentlemen. Don't keep saying, "Woe to us!" [*A car honks offstage.*] Taxi!—Taxi! [*A car stops offstage.*] If you'll excuse me—— [*He hurries off.*

Chorus. Citizen—where to?

The car drives off.

Leader. What is his recourse, poor wretch?
Forceful, yet fearful,
Milk-white of face,
Fearful yet firm—
Against what?

The car is heard honking.

Chorus. So soon accustomed to bad smells!

The car is heard distantly honking.

Woe to us!

Leader. Woe to you!

The CHORUS *retires. All but the* LEADER, *who takes out his
pipe.*

He who dreads action
More than disaster,
How can he fight
When disaster impends?   [*He follows the* CHORUS *out.*

SCENE 5

The Attic. EISENRING *is alone, unwinding cord from a reel and singing "Lily Marlene" while he works. He stops, wets his forefinger, and holds it up to the dormer window to test the wind.*

The Living Room. BIEDERMANN *enters, cigar in mouth, followed by* BABETTE. *He takes off his coat and throws down his brief case.*

BIEDERMANN. Do as I say.

    Babette. A goose?

    Biedermann. A goose! [*He takes off his tie without removing his cigar.*]

    Babette. Why are you taking off your necktie, Gottlieb?

    Biedermann. If I report those two guys to the police, I'll make them my enemies. What good will that do me? Just one match and the whole house is up in flames! What good will that do us? On the other hand, if I go up there and invite them to dinner, why—— ·

    Babette. Why, what?

    Biedermann. Why, then we'll be friends. [*He takes off his jacket, hands it to* BABETTE, *and exits.*]

    Babette [*speaking to* ANNA, *offstage*]. Just so you'll know, Anna: you can't get off this evening—we're having company. Set places for four.

47

The Attic. EISENRING *is singing "Lily Marlene." There is a knock at the door.*

Eisenring. Come in! [*He goes on singing. No one enters.*] Come in! [BIEDERMANN *enters in shirt sleeves, holding his cigar.*] Good day, Mr. Biedermann!

Biedermann [*tactfully*]. May I come in?

Eisenring. I hope you slept well last night?

Biedermann. Thank you—miserably.

Eisenring. So did I. It's this wind. [*He goes on working with the reel.*]

Biedermann. If I'm not disturbing you——

Eisenring. This is your house, Mr. Biedermann.

Biedermann. If I'm not in the way—— [*The cooing of doves is heard.*] Where is our friend?

Eisenring. Sepp? He went to work this morning. The lazy dog—he didn't want to go without breakfast! I sent him out for some sawdust.

Biedermann. Sawdust?

Eisenring. It helps spread the fire. [BIEDERMANN *laughs politely at what sounds like a poor joke.*]

Biedermann. I came up to say, Mr. Eisenring——

Eisenring. That you still want to kick us out?

Biedermann. In the middle of the night—I'm out of sleeping pills—it suddenly struck me: you folks have no toilet facilities up here.

Eisenring. We have the roof gutter.

Biedermann. Well, just as you like, of course. It merely struck me you might like to wash or take a shower—I kept thinking of that all night. . . . You're very welcome to use my bathroom. I told Anna to hang up some towels for you there. [EISENRING *shakes his head.*] Why do you shake your head?

Eisenring. Where on earth did he put it?

Biedermann. What?

Eisenring. You haven't seen a detonator cap? [*He searches around.*] Don't trouble yourself, Mr. Biedermann. In jail, you know, we had no bathrooms either.

Biedermann. In jail?

Eisenring. Didn't Sepp tell you I just came out of prison?

Biedermann. No.

Eisenring. Not a word about it?

Biedermann. No.

Eisenring. All he likes to talk about is himself. There *are* such people!—— Is it our fault, after all, if his youth was tragic? Did *you* have a tragic youth, Mr. Biedermann? I didn't. I could have gone to college; my father wanted me to be a lawyer. . . . [*He stands at the attic window murmuring to the doves.*] Grrr! Grrr! Grrr! [BIEDERMANN *relights his cigar.*]

Biedermann. Frankly, Mr. Eisenring, I couldn't sleep all night. Is there really gasoline in those barrels?

Eisenring. You don't trust us.

Biedermann. I'm merely asking.

Eisenring. Mr. Biedermann, what do you take us for? Frankly, what sort of people——

Biedermann. Mr. Eisenring, you mustn't think I have no sense of humor. Only your idea of a joke—well——

Eisenring. That's something we've learned.

Biedermann. What is?

Eisenring. A joke is good camouflage. Next best comes sentiment: like when Sepp talks about childhood in the coal mines, orphanages, circuses, and so forth. But the best camouflage of all—in my opinion—is the plain and simple truth. Because nobody ever believes it.

The Living Room. ANNA *shows in the* WIDOW KNECHTLING, *dressed in black.*

Anna. Take a seat, please. [*The* WIDOW *sits.*] But if you are Mrs. Knechtling, it's no use. Mr. Biedermann wants nothing to do with you, he said. [*The* WIDOW *gets up.*] Do sit down, please! [*The* WIDOW *sits down again.*] But don't get up any hopes. [ANNA *exits.*

The Attic. EISENRING *busies himself stringing out the fuse.* BIEDERMANN *is smoking.*

Eisenring. I wonder what's keeping Sepp. Sawdust can't be so hard to find. I hope they haven't nabbed him.

Biedermann. Nabbed?

Eisenring. Why do you smile?

Biedermann. When you use words like that, Mr. Eisenring, it's as though you came from another world. Nab him! Like another world! *Our* kind of people seldom get nabbed!

Eisenring. Because your kind of people seldom steal sawdust. That's obvious, Mr. Biedermann. That's the class difference.

Biedermann. Nonsense!

Eisenring. You don't mean to say, Mr. Biedermann——

Biedermann. I don't hold with class differences—you must have realized that by now, Mr. Eisenring. I'm not old-fashioned—just the opposite, in fact. And I regret that the lower classes still talk about class differences. Aren't we all of us—rich or poor—the creation of one Creator? The middle class, too. Are we not—you and I—human beings, made of flesh.

and blood? . . . I don't know, sir, whether you smoke cigars—— [He offers one, but EISENRING shakes his head.] I don't mean reducing people to a common level, understand me. There will always be rich and poor, thank heaven—but why can't we just shake hands? A little good will, for heaven's sake, a little idealism, a little—and we'd all have peace and quiet, both the poor and the rich. Don't you agree?

Eisenring. If I may speak frankly, Mr. Biedermann——

Biedermann. Please do.

Eisenring. You won't take it amiss?

Biedermann. The more frankly the better.

Eisenring. Frankly speaking, you oughtn't to smoke here.

[BIEDERMANN, startled, puts out his cigar.] I can't make rules for you here, Mr. Biedermann. After all, it's your house. Still and all——

Biedermann. Of course.

Eisenring [looking down]. There it is! [He takes something off the floor and blows it clean before attaching it to the fuse. He starts whistling "Lily Marlene."]

Biedermann. Tell me, Mr. Eisenring, what is that you're doing? If I may ask? What is that thing?

Eisenring. A detonator.

Biedermann. A ——?

Eisenring. And this is a fuse.

Biedermann. A ——?

Eisenring. Sepp says they've developed better ones lately. But they're not for sale to the public. Anyway buying them's out of the question for us. Anything that has to do with war is frightfully expensive. Always the best quality . . .

Biedermann. A fuse, you say?

Eisenring. A time fuse. [*He hands* BIEDERMANN *one end of the cord.*] If you'd be kind enough, Mr. Biedermann, to hold this end—— [BIEDERMANN *holds it for him.*]

Biedermann. All joking aside, my friend——

Eisenring. One second—— [*He whistles "Lily Marlene," measuring the fuse.*] Thank you, Mr. Biedermann. [BIEDER-MANN *suddenly laughs.*]

Biedermann. Ha, ha! You can't put a scare into me, Willi! Though I must say, you do count on people's sense of humor. The way you talk, I can understand your getting arrested now and then. You know, not everybody has my sense of humor!

Eisenring. You have to find the right man.

Biedermann. At the pub, for instance—just say you believe in the natural goodness of man, and they have you marked down.

Eisenring. Ha! [*He puts down the fuse.*] Those who have no sense of humor get what's coming to them just the same when the time comes—so don't let *that* worry you. [BIEDER-MANN *sits down on a barrel. He has broken into a sweat.*] What's the trouble, Mr. Biedermann? You've gone quite pale. [*He claps him on the shoulder.*] It's the smell. I know, if you're not used to it . . . I'll open the window for you, too. [*He opens the door.*]

Biedermann. Thanks . . . [ANNA *calls up the stairs.*]

Anna's Voice. Mr. Biedermann! Mr. Biedermann!

Eisenring. The police again? It's a Police State!

Anna's Voice. Mr. Biedermann——

Biedermann. I'm coming! [*They both whisper from here on.*] Mr. Eisenring, do you like goose?

Eisenring. Goose?

Biedermann. Roast goose.

Eisenring. Why?

Biedermann. Stuffed with chestnuts?

Eisenring. And red cabbage?

Biedermann. Yes . . . I was going to say: my wife and I—I, especially—if we may have the pleasure . . . I don't mean to intrude, Mr. Eisenring, but if you'd care to join us at a little supper, you and Sepp——

Eisenring. Today?

Biedermann. Or tomorrow, if you prefer——

Eisenring. We probably won't stay until tomorrow. But today—of course, Mr. Biedermann, with pleasure.

Biedermann. Shall we say seven o'clock? [*They shake hands.* BIEDERMANN *at the door.*] Is it a date? [*He nods genially, then stares once more at the barrels and the fuse.*]

Eisenring. It's a date.

BIEDERMANN *exits.* EISENRING *goes to work again, whistling. The* CHORUS *enters below as if for the end of the scene. They are interrupted by the sound of a crash, of something falling in the attic.*

Eisenring. You can come out, Professor. [*A* PH.D., *wearing horn-rimmed glasses, crawls out from behind the barrels.*] You heard: we're invited to dinner, Sepp and me. You'll keep an eye on things. Nobody's to come in here and smoke, understand? Not before we're ready. [*The* PH.D. *polishes his glasses.*] I often ask myself, Professor, why in hell you hang around with us. You don't enjoy a good, crackling fire, or flames, or sparks. Or sirens that go off too late—or dogs barking—or people shrieking—or smoke. Or ashes . . . [*The* PH.D. *solemnly adjusts his glasses.* EISENRING *laughs.*] Do-gooder! [*He whistles gently to himself, surveying the professor.*] I don't like you eggheads—I've told you that before, Professor. You get no real fun out of anything. You're all so idealistic, so solemn. . . . Until you're ready to betray. That's no fun either, Professor. [*He goes back to his work, whistling.*]

Downstairs.

Chorus. Ready for action,
    Axes and fire hose;
    Polished and oiled,
    Every brass fitting.
    Every man of us tested and ready.

Leader. We'll be facing a high wind.

Chorus. Every man of us tested and ready.
    Our brass fire pump
    Polished and oiled,
    Tested for pressure.

Leader. And the fire hydrants?

Chorus. Everything ready.

Leader. Tested and ready for action.

Enter BABETTE *with a goose, and the* PH.D.

Babette. Yes, Professor, I know, but my husband . . . Yes, I understand it's urgent, Professor. I'll tell him—— [*She leaves the professor and comes to the footlights.*] My husband ordered a goose. See, this is it. And I have to roast it, so we can be friends with those people upstairs. [*Churchbells ring.*] It's Saturday night—you can hear the bells ringing. I have an odd feeling, somehow, that it may be the last time we'll hear them. [BIEDERMANN *calls,* "Babette!"] I don't know, ladies, if Gottlieb is always right. . . . You know what he says? "Certainly they're scoundrels, Babette, but if I make enemies of them, it's goodbye to our hair tonic!" [BIEDER-MANN *calls,* "Babette!"] Gottlieb's like that. Good-hearted. Always too good-hearted! [*She exits with the goose.*]

Chorus. This son of good family,
 A wearer of glasses,
 Pale, studious, trusting,
 But trusting no longer
 In power of goodness,
 Will do anything now, for
 Ends justify means.
 (So he hopes.)
 Ah, honest-dishonest!
 Now wiping his glasses
 To see things more clearly,
 He sees no barrels—
 No gasoline barrels!
 It's an idea he sees—
 An abstract conception—
 Until it explodes!

Ph.D. Good evening . . .

Leader. To the pumps!
 The ladders!
 The engines!

> *The firemen rush to their posts.*

Leader. Good evening. [*To the audience, as shouts of*
 "Ready!" *echo through the theatre.*]
 We're ready.

SCENE 6

The Living Room. The WIDOW KNECHTLING *is still there waiting. Outside, the bells are ringing loudly.* ANNA *is setting the table.* BIEDERMANN *brings in two chairs.*

BIEDERMANN. You can see, can't you, Mrs. Knechtling? I haven't time now—no time to think about the dead. . . . I told you, go see my lawyer. [*The* WIDOW KNECHTLING *leaves.*] You can't hear yourself think, with that noise. Close the window. [ANNA *shuts the window. The sound of the bells is fainter.*] I said a simple, informal dinner. What are those idiotic candelabra for?

Anna. But, Mr. Biedermann, we always have those!

Biedermann. I said simple, informal—no ostentation. Fingerbowls! Knife-rests! Nothing but crystal and silver! What are you trying to do? [*He picks up the knife-rests and shoves them into his pants pocket.*] Can't you see I'm wearing my oldest jacket? And you . . . leave the carving knife, Anna —we'll need it; but away with the rest of this silver! Those two gentlemen must feel at home!—— Where's the corkscrew?

Anna. Here.

Biedermann. Don't we have anything simpler?

Anna. In the kitchen. But that one is rusty.

Biedermann. Bring it here. [*He takes a silver ice bucket off the table.*] What's this for?

Anna. For the wine.

Biedermann. Silver! [*He glares at the bucket, then at* ANNA.] Do we always use that, too?

Anna. We're going to need it, Mr. Biedermann.

Biedermann. Humanity, brotherhood—that's what we need here! Away with that thing! And what are those, will you tell me?

Anna. Napkins.

Biedermann. Damask napkins!

Anna. We don't have any others. [BIEDERMANN *shoves the napkins into the silver bucket.*]

Biedermann. There are whole nations, Anna, that live without napkins! [BABETTE *enters with a large wreath.* BIEDERMANN, *standing in front of the table, does not see her come in.*] And why a cloth on the table?

Babette. Gottlieb?

Biedermann. Let's have no class distinctions! [*He sees* BABETTE.] What is that wreath?

Babette. It's what we ordered—— Gottlieb, what do you think? They sent the wreath here by mistake! And I gave them the address myself—Knechtling's address—I wrote it down, even! And the ribbon and everything—they've got it all backward!

Biedermann. What's wrong with the ribbon?

Babette. And the clerk says they sent the bill to Mrs. Knechtling! [*She shows him the ribbon.*] "To Our Dear, Departed Gottlieb Biedermann." [*He considers the ribbon.*]

Biedermann. We won't accept it, that's all! I should say not! They've got to exchange it! [*He goes back to the table.*] Don't upset me, will you, Babette? I can't think of everything——

BABETTE *exits.*

Biedermann. Take that tablecloth away. Help me, Anna. And remember—no serving! You come in and put the pan on the table.

Anna. The roasting pan?! [*He takes off the tablecloth.*]

Biedermann. That's better! Just a bare table, for a plain and simple supper. [*He hands* ANNA *the tablecloth.*]

Anna. You mean that, Mr. Biedermann—just bring in the goose in the pan? [*She folds up the tablecloth.*] What wine shall I bring?

Biedermann. I'll get it myself.

Anna. Mr. Biedermann!

Biedermann. What now?

Anna. I don't have any sweater, sir—any old sweater, as if I belonged to the family.

Biedermann. Borrow one of my wife's.

Anna. The yellow or the red one?

Biedermann. Don't make a fuss! No apron or cap, understand? And get rid of these candelabra. And make sure especially, Anna, that everything's not so neat!—I'll be in the cellar.   [BIEDERMANN *exits.*

Anna. "Make sure especially, Anna, that everything's not so neat!" [*She throws the tablecloth down on the floor and stomps on it with both feet.*] How's that?

SCHMITZ *and* EISENRING *enter, each holding a rose.*

Both. Good evening, miss.

ANNA *exits without looking at them.*

Eisenring. Why no sawdust?

Schmitz. Confiscated. Police measure. Precaution. They're picking up anybody who sells or owns sawdust without written permission. Precautions all over the place. [*He combs his hair.*]

Eisenring. Have you got matches?

Schmitz. No.

Eisenring. Neither have I. [SCHMITZ *blows his comb clean.*]

Schmitz. We'll have to ask him for them.

Eisenring. Biedermann?

Schmitz. Don't forget. [*He puts away his comb and sniffs.*] Mmm! That smells good!

SCENE 7

BIEDERMANN *comes to the footlights with a bottle.*

BIEDERMANN. You can think what you like about me, gentlemen. But just answer one question—— [*Laughter and loud
voices offstage.*] I say to myself: as long as they're laughing
and drinking, we're safe. The best bottles out of my cellar!
I tell you, if anybody had told me a week ago . . . When
did *you* guess they were arsonists, gentlemen? This sort of
thing doesn't happen the way you think. It comes on you
slowly—slowly, at first—then sudden suspicion! Though I
was suspicious at once—one's always suspicious! But tell
me the truth, sirs—what would *you* have done? If you were
in my place, for God's sake? And when? *When* would you
have done it? At what point? [*He waits for an answer. Silence.*] I must go back up. [*He leaves the stage quickly.*]

SCENE 8

The Living Room. The dinner is in full swing. Laughter. Biedermann, *especially, cannot contain himself at the joke he's
just heard. Only* Babette *is not laughing.*

Biedermann. Oil waste! Did you hear that, Babette? Oil
waste, he says! Oil waste burns better!

Babette. I don't see what's funny.

Biedermann. Oil waste! You know what that is?

Babette. Yes.

Biedermann. You have no sense of humor, Babette. [*He
puts the bottle on the table.*]

Babette. All right, then, explain it.

Biedermann. Okay!—— This morning Willi told Sepp to
go out and steal some sawdust. Sawdust—get it? And just
now, when I asked Sepp if he got any, he said he couldn't find
any sawdust—he found some oil waste instead. Get it? And
Willi says, "Oil waste burns better!"

Babette. I understood all that.

Biedermann. You did?

Babette. What's funny about it? [Biedermann *gives up.*]

Biedermann. Let's drink, men! [Biedermann *removes the
cork from the bottle.*]

Babette. Is that the truth, Mr. Schmitz? Did you bring
oil waste up to our attic?

Biedermann. This will kill you, Babette! This morning we
even measured the fuse together, Willi and I!

69

Babette. The fuse?

Biedermann The time fuse. [*He fills the glasses.*]

Babette. Seriously—what does that mean? [BIEDERMANN *laughs.*]

Biedermann. Seriously! You hear that? Seriously! . . . Don't let them kid you, Babette. I told you—our friends have their own way of kidding! Different company, different jokes —that's what I always say. . . . All we need now is to have them ask me for matches! [SCHMITZ *and* EISENRING *exchange glances.*] These gentlemen took me for some Milquetoast, for some dope without humor—— [*He lifts his glass.*] Prosit!

Eisenring. Prosit!

Schmitz. Prosit!

Biedermann. To our friendship! [*They drink the toast standing up, then sit down again.*] We're not doing any serving. Just help yourselves, gentlemen.

Schmitz. I can't eat any more.

Eisenring. Don't restrain yourself, Sepp, you're not at the orphanage. [*He helps himself to more goose.*] Your goose is wonderful, madam.

Babette. I'm glad to hear it.

Eisenring. Roast goose and stuffing! Now all we need is a tablecloth.

Babette. You hear that, Gottlieb?

Eisenring. We don't have to have one. But one of those tablecloths, white damask, with silverware on it——

Biedermann [*loudly*]. Anna!

Eisenring. Damask, with flowers all over it—a white flower pattern—we don't have to have one. We didn't have any in prison.

Babette. In prison?

Biedermann. Where is that girl?

Babette. Have you been in prison?

ANNA *enters. She is wearing a bright red sweater.*

Biedermann. A tablecloth here—immediately!

Anna. Yes sir.

Biedermann. And if you have some fingerbowls or something——

Anna. Yes sir.

Eisenring. Madam, you may think it's childish, but that's how the little man is. Take Sepp, for instance—he grew up in the coal mines, but it's the dream of his miserable life, a table like this, with crystal and silver! Would you believe it? He never heard of a knife-rest!

Babette. But, Gottlieb, we have all those things!

Eisenring. Of course we don't *have* to have them here——

Anna. Very well.

Eisenring. If you have any napkins, miss, out with them!

Anna. But Mr. Biedermann said——

Biedermann. Out with them!

Anna. Yes sir. [*She starts to bring back the table service.*]

Eisenring. I hope you won't take it amiss, madam, but when you're just out of prison—months at a time with no refinement whatever—— [*He shows the tablecloth to* SCHMITZ.] You know what this is? [*To* BABETTE.] He never saw one before! [*He turns back to* SCHMITZ.] This is damask!

Schmitz. What do you want me to do with it? [EISENRING *ties the tablecloth around* SCHMITZ's *neck.*]

Eisenring. There—— [BIEDERMANN *tries to find this amusing. He laughs.*]

Babette. Where are the knife-rests, Anna?

Anna. Mr. Biedermann——

Biedermann. Out with them!

Anna. But you said "Take them away!" before!

Biedermann. Bring them here, I tell you! Where are they, goddammit?

Anna. In your pants pocket. [BIEDERMANN *reaches in his pants pocket and finds them.*]

Eisenring. Don't get excited.

Anna. I can't help it!

Eisenring. No excitement, now miss—— [ANNA *bursts into sobs and runs out.*]

Eisenring. It's this wind. [*Pause.*]

Biedermann. Drink up, friends! [*They drink. A silence.*]

Eisenring. I ate roast goose every day when I was a waiter. I used to flit down those corridors holding a platter like this. . . . How do you suppose, madam, waiters clean off their hands? In their hair, that's how—while there's others who use crystal fingerbowls. That's something I'll never forget. [*He dips his fingers in the fingerbowl.*] Have you ever heard of a trauma?

Biedermann. No.

Eisenring. I learned all about it in jail. [*He wipes his fingers dry.*]

Babette. And how did you happen to be there, Mr. Eisenring?

Biedermann. Babette!

Eisenring. How did I get into jail?

Biedermann. One doesn't ask questions like that!

Eisenring. I wonder at that myself. . . . I was a waiter—a little headwaiter. Suddenly they made me out a great arsonist.

Biedermann. Hm.

Eisenring. They called for me at my own home.

Biedermann. Hm.

Eisenring. I was so amazed, I played along.

Biedermann. Hm.

Eisenring. I had luck, madam—seven really charming policemen. I said, "I have no time—I have to go to work." They answered, "Your restaurant's burned to the ground."

Biedermann. Burned to the ground?

Eisenring. Overnight, apparently.

Babette. Burned to the ground?

Eisenring. "Fine," I said. "Then I *have* time. . . ." Just a black, smoking hulk—that's all that was left of that place. I saw it as we drove by. Through those windows, you know, the little barred windows they have in those prison vans—— [*He sips his wine delicately.*]

Biedermann. And then? [EISENRING *studies the wine label.*]

Eisenring. We used to keep this, too: '49, Cave de l'Echannon . . . And then? Let Sepp tell you the rest—— As I was sitting in that police station, playing with my handcuffs, who do you think they brought in?—— That one, there! [SCHMITZ *beams.*] *Prosit*, Sepp!

Schmitz. Prosit, Willi! [*They drink.*]

Biedermann. And then?

Schmitz. "Are you a firebug?" they asked him, and offered him cigarettes. He said, "Excuse me, I have no matches, Mr. Commissioner, although you think I'm a firebug——" [*They laugh uproariously and slap each other's thighs.*]

Biedermann. Hm.

ANNA *enters, in cap and apron again. She hands* BIEDERMANN
a visiting card.

Anna. It's urgent, he says.

Biedermann. When I have visitors—— [SCHMITZ *and*
EISENRING *clink glasses again.*]

Schmitz. Prosit, Willi!

Eisenring. Prosit, Sepp! [*They drink.* BIEDERMANN *studies
the visiting card.*]

Babette. Who is it, Gottlieb?

Biedermann. It's some PH.D. . . . [ANNA *is busy at the
sideboard.*]

Eisenring. And what are those other things, miss—those
silver things?

Anna. The candlesticks?

Eisenring. Why do you hide them?

Biedermann. Bring them here!

Anna. But you said, yourself, Mr. Biedermann——

Biedermann. I say bring them here! [ANNA *places the candelabra on the table.*]

Eisenring. What do you say to that, Sepp? They have
candlesticks and they hide them! Real silver candlesticks—
what more do you want?—— Have you a match? [*He reaches
into his pants pocket.*]

Schmitz. Me? No. [*He reaches into his pants pocket.*]

Eisenring. Sorry, no matches, Mr. Biedermann.

Biedermann. I have some.

Eisenring. Let's have them.

Biedermann. I'll light the candles. Let me—I'll do it. [*He
begins lighting the candles.*]

Babette [*to* ANNA]. What does the visitor want?

Anna. I don't know, ma'am. He says he can no longer be silent. And he's waiting on the stoop.

Babette. It's private, he says?

Anna. Yes ma'am. He says he wants to expose something.

Babette. Expose something?!

Anna. That's what he keeps saying. I don't understand him. He wants to dissociate himself, he says. . . . [BIEDERMANN *is still lighting candles.*]

Eisenring. It creates an atmosphere, doesn't it, madam? Candlelight, I mean.

Babette. Yes, it does.

Eisenring. I'm all for atmosphere. Refined, candlelight atmosphere——

Biedermann. I'm happy to know that. [*All the candles are lit.*]

Eisenring. Schmitz, don't smack your lips when you eat! [BABETTE *takes* EISENRING *aside.*]

Babette. Let him alone!

Eisenring. He has no manners, madam. Excuse me—it's awful. But where could he have picked up any manners? From the coal mines to the orphanage——

Babette. I know.

Eisenring. From the orphanage to the circus.

Babette. I know.

Eisenring. From the circus to the theatre——

Babette. I didn't know.

Eisenring. A football of fate, madam. [BABETTE *turns to* SCHMITZ.]

Babette. In the theatre! Were you, really? [Schmitz *gnaws on a drumstick and nods.*] Where?

Schmitz. Upstage.

Eisenring. Really talented, too! Sepp as a ghost! Can you imagine it?

Schmitz. Not any more, though.

Eisenring. Why not?

Schmitz. I was in the theatre only a week, madam, before it burned to the ground.

Babette. Burned to the ground?

Eisenring [*to* Schmitz]. Don't be diffident!

Biedermann. Burned to the ground?

Eisenring. Don't be so diffident! [*He unties the tablecloth* Schmitz *has been wearing and throws it over* Schmitz's *head.*] Come on! [Schmitz *gets up with the tablecloth over him.*] Doesn't he look like a ghost?

Anna. I'm frightened!

Eisenring. Come here, little girl! [*He pulls* Anna *onto his lap. She hides her face in her hands.*]

Schmitz. Who calleth?

Eisenring. That's theatre language, madam. They call that a cue. He learned it in less than a week, before the theatre burned down.

Babette. Please don't keep talking of fires!

Schmitz. Who calleth?

Eisenring. Ready—— [*Everybody waits expectantly.* Eisenring *has a tight grip on* Anna.]

Schmitz. EVERYMAN! EVERYMAN!

Babette. Gottlieb?

Biedermann. Quiet!

Babette. We saw that in Salzburg!

Schmitz. BIEDERMANN! BIEDERMANN!

Eisenring. He's terrific!

Schmitz. BIEDERMANN! BIEDERMANN!

Eisenring. You must say, "Who are you?"

Biedermann. Me?

Eisenring. Or he can't say his lines.

Schmitz. EVERYMAN! BIEDERMANN!

Biedermann. All right, then—who am I?

Babette. No! You must ask him who *he* is.

Biedermann. I see.

Schmitz. DOST THOU HEAR ME?

Eisenring. No, no, Sepp—start it again. [*They change their positions.*]

Schmitz. EVERYMAN! BIEDERMANN!

Babette. Are you the Angel of Death, maybe?

Biedermann. Nonsense!

Babette. What else *could* he be?

Biedermann. Ask him. He might be the ghost in *Hamlet.* Or that other one—what's-his-name—in *Macbeth.*

Schmitz. WHO CALLS ME?

Eisenring. Go on.

Schmitz. GOTTLIEB BIEDERMANN!

Babette. Go ahead, ask him. He's talking to you.

Schmitz. DOST THOU HEAR ME?

Biedermann. Who are you?

Schmitz. I AM THE GHOST OF—KNECHTLING. [*He throws the tablecloth over* BIEDERMANN. BABETTE *jumps up with a scream.*]

Eisenring. Stop! [*He pulls the tablecloth off* BIEDERMANN.] Idiot! How could you do such a thing? Knechtling was buried today!

Schmitz. That's why I thought of him. [BABETTE *hides her face in her hands.*]

Eisenring. He's not Knechtling, madam. [*He shakes his head over* SCHMITZ.] What crudeness!

Schmitz. He was on my mind.

Eisenring. Of all things—Knechtling! Mr. Biedermann's best old employee! Imagine it: buried today—cold and stiff— not yet moldy—pale as this tablecloth—white and shiny as damask—— To go and act Knechtling—— [*He takes* BA- BETTE *by the shoulder.*] Honest to God, madam, it's Sepp— it's not Knechtling at all. [SCHMITZ *wipes off his sweat.*]

Schmitz. I'm sorry. . . .

Biedermann. Let's sit down again.

Anna. Is it over?

Biedermann. Would you care for cigars, sirs? [*He offers a box of cigars.*]

Eisenring [*to* SCHMITZ]. Idiot! You see how Mr. Bieder- mann is shaking! . . . Thank you, Mr. Biedermann!—— You think that's funny, Sepp? When you know very well that Knechtling put his head inside the gas stove? After every- thing Gottlieb did for him? He gave this Knechtling a job for fourteen years—and this is his thanks!

Biedermann. Let's not talk about it.

Eisenring [*to* SCHMITZ]. And that's your thanks for the goose! [*They attend to their cigars.*]

Schmitz. Would you like me to sing something?

Eisenring. What?

Schmitz. "Fox, you stole that lovely goosie . . . [*He sings loudly.*]
> Fox, you stole that lovely goosie,
> Give it back again!"

Eisenring. That's enough.

Schmitz. "Give it back again!
> Or they'll get you in the shnoosie——"

Eisenring. He's drunk.

Schmitz. "With their shooting gun!"

Eisenring. Pay no attention to him.

Schmitz. "Give it back again!
> Or they'll get you in the shnoosie
> With their shooting gun!"

Biedermann. "Shooting gun!" That's good!

                The Men all join in the song.

The Men. "Fox, you stole that lovely goosie . . ."

They harmonize, now loudly, now softly. Laughter and loud cheer. There is a pause, and BIEDERMANN *picks up again, leading the hilarity until they've all had it.*

Biedermann. So—— Prosit! [*They raise their glasses. Fire sirens are heard nearby.*] What was that?

Eisenring. Sirens.

Biedermann. Joking aside——

Babette. Firebugs! Firebugs!

Biedermann. Don't yell like that!

BABETTE *runs to the window and throws it open. The sound of the sirens comes nearer, with a howl that goes to the marrow. The fire engines roar past.*

Biedermann. At least it's not here.

Babette. I wonder where?

Eisenring. From where the wind is blowing.

Biedermann. Not here, anyway.

Eisenring. That's how we generally work it. Lure the Fire Department out to some suburb or other, and then, when things really let loose, they find their way back blocked.

Biedermann. No, gentlemen—all joking aside——

Schmitz. That's how we do it—joking aside——

Biedermann. Please—enough of this nonsense! Don't overdo it! Look at my wife—white as chalk!

Babette. And you too!

Biedermann. Besides, a fire alarm is nothing to laugh at, gentlemen. Somewhere some place is burning, or the Fire Department wouldn't be rushing there. [EISENRING *looks at his watch.*]

Eisenring. We've got to go now.

Biedermann. Now?

Eisenring. Sorry.

Schmitz. "Or they'll get you in the shnoosie . . ." [*The sirens are heard again.*]

Biedermann. Bring us some coffee, Babette! [BABETTE *goes out.*] And you, Anna—do you have to stand there and gape? [ANNA *goes out.*] Just between us, gentlemen: enough is enough. My wife has a heart condition. Let's have no more joking about fires.

Schmitz. We're not joking, Mr. Biedermann.

Eisenring. We're firebugs.

Biedermann. No, gentlemen, quite seriously——

Eisenring. Quite seriously.

Schmitz. Yeah, quite seriously. Why don't you believe us?

Eisenring. Your house is very favorably situated, Mr. Biedermann, you must admit that. Five villas like yours around the gasworks. . . . It's true they keep a close watch on the gasworks. Still, there's a good stiff wind blowing——

Biedermann. It can't be——

Schmitz. Let's have plain talk! You think we're firebugs——

Biedermann [*like a whipped dog*]. No, no, I don't think you are! You do me an injustice, gentlemen—I don't think you're firebugs. . . .

Eisenring. You swear you don't?

Biedermann. No! No! No! I don't believe it!

Schmitz. What *do* you think we are?

Biedermann. You're my friends. . . . [*They clap him on the shoulder and start to leave.*]

Eisenring. It's time to leave.

Biedermann. Gentlemen, I swear to you by all that's holy——

Eisenring. By all that's holy?

Biedermann. Yes. [*He raises his hand as though to take an oath.*]

Schmitz. Willi doesn't believe in anything holy, Mr. Biedermann. Any more than you do. You'll waste your time swearing. [*They go to the door.*]

Biedermann. What can I do to make you believe me? [*He blocks the doorway.*]

Eisenring. Give us some matches.

Biedermann. Some——

Eisenring. We have no more matches.

Biedermann. You want me to——

Eisenring. If you don't think we're firebugs.

Biedermann. Matches——

Schmitz. To show your belief in us, he means. [BIEDER
MANN *reaches in his pocket.*]

Eisenring. See how he hesitates?

Biedermann. Sh! Not in front of my wife . . .

BABETTE *returns.*

Babette. Your coffee will be ready in a minute. [*Pause.*]
Must you go?

Biedermann [*formally*]. At least you've felt, while here,
my friends . . . I don't want to make a speech on this occa-
sion, but may we not drink, before you go, to our eternal
friendship? [*He picks up a bottle and the corkscrew.*]

Eisenring. Tell your very charming husband, madam, that
he needn't open any more bottles on our account. It isn't
worth the trouble any more.

Biedermann. It's no trouble, my friends, no trouble at all.
If there's anything else you'd like—anything at all—— [*He
fills the glasses once more and hands them out.*] My friends!
[*They clink glasses.*] Sepp—— Willi—— [*He kisses them
each on the cheek. All drink.*]

Eisenring. Just the same, we must go now.

Schmitz. Unfortunately.

Eisenring. Madam—— [*Sirens.*]

Babette. It's been such a nice evening. [*Alarm bells.*]

Eisenring. Just one thing, now, Gottlieb——

Biedermann. What is it?

Eisenring. I've mentioned it to you before.

Biedermann. Anything you like. Just name it.

Eisenring. The matches.

Anna has entered with coffee.

Babette. Why, what is it, Anna?

Anna. The coffee.

Babette. You're all upset, Anna!

Anna. Back there—Mrs. Biedermann—the sky! You can see it from the kitchen—the whole sky is burning, Mrs. Biedermann!

The scene is turning red as Schmitz *and* Eisenring *make their bows and exit.* Biedermann *is left pale and shaken.*

Biedermann. Not our house, fortunately . . . Not our house . . . Not our . . . [*The* Ph.D. *enters.*] Who are you, and what do you want?

Ph.D. I can no longer be silent. [*He takes out a paper and reads.*] "Cognizant of the events now transpiring, whose iniquitous nature must be readily apparent, the undersigned submits to the authorities the subsequent statement . . ." [*Amid the shrieking of sirens he reads an involved statement, of which no one understands a word. Dogs howl, bells ring, there is the scream of departing sirens and the crackling of flames. The* Ph.D. *hands* Biedermann *the paper.*] I disassociate myself. . . .

Biedermann. But——

Ph.D. I have said my say. [*He takes off and folds up his glasses.* You see, Mr. Biedermann, I was intent on improving the world; I knew about everything they were doing in your attic, everything. The one thing I didn't know was this: They—they are doing it for the pure joy of it.

Biedermann. Professor—— [*The* Ph.D. *removes himself.*] What will I do with this, Professor?

The Ph.D. *climbs over the footlights and takes a seat in the*
audience.

Babette. Gottlieb——

Biedermann. He's gone.

Babette. What did you give them? Matches? Not matches?

Biedermann. Why not?

Babette. Not matches?

Biedermann. If they really were firebugs, do you think
they wouldn't have matches? Don't be foolish, Babette!

The clock strikes. Silence. The red light onstage begins
deepening into blackness. Sirens. Bells ring. Dogs howl. Cars
honk. . . . A crash of collapsing buildings. A crackling of
flames. Screams and outcries . . . fading. The Chorus
comes on again.

Chorus. Useless, quite useless.
   And nothing more useless
   Than this useless story.
   For arson, once kindled,
   Kills many,
   Leaves few,
   And accomplishes nothing.

First detonation.

Leader. That was the gasworks.

Second detonation.

Chorus. Long foreseen, disaster
   Has reached us at last.
   Horrendous arson!
   Unquenchable fire.
   Fate—so they call it!

Third detonation.

Leader. More gas tanks.

There is a series of frightful explosions.

Chorus. Woe to us! Woe to us! Woe!

The house lights go up.
Curtain.

DRAMABOOKS
(Plays)

MERMAID DRAMABOOKS

Christopher Marlowe (Tamburlaine the Great, Parts I & II, Doctor Faustus, The Jew of Malta, Edward the Second) (0701-0)

William Congreve (Complete Plays) (0702-9)

Webster and Tourneur (The White Devil, The Duchess of Malfi, The Atheist's Tragedy, The Revenger's Tragedy) (0703-7)

John Ford (The Lover's Melancholy, 'Tis Pity She's a Whore, The Broken Heart, Love's Sacrifice, Perkin Warbeck) (0704-5)

Richard Brinsley Sheridan (The Rivals, St. Patrick's Day, The Duenna, A Trip to Scarborough, The School for Scandal, The Critic) (0705-3)

Camille and Other Plays (Scribe: A Peculiar Position, The Glass of Water; Sardou: A Scrap of Paper; Dumas: Camille; Augier: Olympe's Marriage) (0706-1)

John Dryden (The Conquest of Granada, Parts I & II, Marriage à la Mode, Aureng-Zebe) (0707-X)

Ben Jonson Vol. 1 (Volpone, Epicoene, The Alchemist) (0708-8)

Oliver Goldsmith (The Good Natur'd Man, She Stoops to Conquer, An Essay on the Theatre, A Register of Scotch Marriages) (0709-6)

Jean Anouilh Vol. 1 (Antigone, Eurydice, The Rehearsal, Romeo and Jeannette, The Ermine) (0710-X)

Let's Get a Divorce! and Other Plays (Labiche: A Trip Abroad, and Célimare; Sardou: Let's Get a Divorce!; Courteline: These Cornfields; Feydeau: Keep an Eye on Amélie; Prévert: A United Family; Achard: Essays on Feydeau) (0711-8)

Jean Giraudoux Vol. 1 (Ondine, The Enchanted, The Madwoman of Chaillot, The Apollo of Bellac) (0712-6)

Jean Anouilh Vol. 2 (Restless Heart, Time Remembered, Ardèle, Mademoiselle Colombe, The Lark) (0713-4)

Henrik Ibsen: The Last Plays (Little Eyolf, John Gabriel Borkman, When We Dead Awaken) (0714-2)

Ivan Turgenev (A Month in the Country, A Provincial Lady, A Poor Gentleman) (0715-0)

George Farquhar (The Constant Couple, The Twin-Rivals, The Recruiting Officer, The Beaux Stratagem) (0716-9)

Jean Racine (Andromache, Britannicus, Berenice, Phaedra, Athaliah) (0717-7)

The Storm and Other Russian Plays (The Storm, The Government Inspector, The Power of Darkness, Uncle Vanya, The Lower Depths) (0718-5)

Michel de Ghelderode: Seven Plays Vol. 1 (The Ostend Interviews, Chronicles of Hell, Barabbas, The Women at the Tomb, Pantagleize, The Blind Men, Three Players and a Play, Lord Halewyn) (0719-3)

Lope de Vega: Five Plays (Peribáñez, Fuenteovejuna, The Dog in the Manger, The Knight from Olmedo, Justice Without Revenge) (0720-7)

Calderón: Four Plays (Secret Vengeance for Secret Insult, Devotion to the Cross, The Mayor of Zalamea, The Phantom Lady) (0721-5)

Jean Cocteau: Five Plays (Orphée, Antigone, Intimate Relations, The Holy Terrors, The Eagle with Two Heads) (0722-3)

Ben Jonson Vol. 2 (Every Man in His Humour, Sejanus, Bartholomew Fair) (0723-1)

Port-Royal and Other Plays (Claudel: Tobias and Sara; Mauriac: Asmodée; Copeau: The Poor Little Man; Montherlant: Port-Royal) (0724-X)

Edwardian Plays (Maugham: Loaves and Fishes; Hankin: The Return of the Prodigal; Shaw: Getting Married; Pinero: Mid-Channel; Granville-Barker: The Madras House) (0725-8)

Alfred de Musset: Seven Plays (0726-6)

Georg Büchner: Complete Plays and Prose (0727-4)

Paul Green: Five Plays (Johnny Johnson, In Abraham's Bosom, Hymn to the Rising Sun, The House of Connelly, White Dresses) (0728-2)

François Billetdoux: Two Plays (Tchin-Tchin, Chez Torpe) (0729-0)

Michel de Ghelderode: Seven Plays Vol. 2 (Red Magic, Hop, Signor!, The Death of Doctor Faust, Christopher Columbus, A Night of Pity, Piet Bouteille, Miss Jairus) (0730-4)

Jean Giraudoux Vol. 2 (Siegfried, Amphitryon 38, Electra) (0731-2)

Kelly's Eye and Other Plays by Henry Livings (Kelly's Eye, Big Soft Nellie, There's No Room for You Here for a Start) (0732-0)

Gabriel Marcel: Three Plays (Man of God, Ariadne, Votive Candle) (0733-9)

New American Plays Vol. 1 ed. by Robert W. Corrigan (0734-7)

Elmer Rice: Three Plays (Adding Machine, Street Scene, Dream Girl) (0735-5)
The Day the Whores Came Out to Play Tennis . . . by Arthur Kopit (0736-3)
Platonov by Anton Chekhov (0737-1)
Ugo Betti: Three Plays (The Inquiry, Goat Island, The Gambler) (0738-X)
Jean Anouilh Vol. 3 (Thieves' Carnival, Medea, Cécile, Traveler Without Luggage, Orchestra, Episode in the Life of an Author, Catch As Catch Can) (0739-8)
Max Frisch: Three Plays (Don Juan, The Great Rage of Philip Hotz, When the War Was Over) (0740-1)
New American Plays Vol. 2 ed. by William M. Hoffman (0741-X)
Plays from Black Africa ed. by Fredric M. Litto (0742-8)
Anton Chekhov: Four Plays (The Seagull, Uncle Vanya, The Cherry Orchard, The Three Sisters) (0743-6)
The Silver Foxes Are Dead and Other Plays by Jakov Lind (The Silver Foxes Are Dead, Anna Laub, Hunger, Fear) (0744-4)
New American Plays Vol. 3 ed. by William M. Hoffman (0745-2)

THE NEW MERMAIDS

Bussy D'Ambois by George Chapman (1101-8)
The Broken Heart by John Ford (1102-6)
The Duchess of Malfi by John Webster (1103-4)
Doctor Faustus by Christopher Marlowe (1104-2)
The Alchemist by Ben Jonson (1105-0)
The Jew of Malta by Christopher Marlowe (1106-9)
The Revenger's Tragedy by Cyril Tourneur (1107-7)
A Game at Chess by Thomas Middleton (1108-5)
Every Man in His Humour by Ben Jonson (1109-3)
The White Devil by John Webster (1110-7)
Edward the Second by Christopher Marlowe (1111-5)
The Malcontent by John Marston (1112-3)
'Tis Pity She's a Whore by John Ford (1113-1)
Sejanus His Fall by Ben Jonson (1114-X)
Volpone by Ben Jonson (1115-8)
Women Beware Women by Thomas Middleton (1116-6)

SPOTLIGHT DRAMABOOKS

The Last Days of Lincoln by Mark Van Doren (1201-4)
Oh Dad, Poor Dad . . . by Arthur Kopit (1202-2)
The Chinese Wall by Max Frisch (1203-0)
Billy Budd by Louis O. Coxe and Robert Chapman (1204-9)
The Devils by John Whiting (1205-7)
The Firebugs by Max Frisch (1206-5)
Andorra by Max Frisch (1207-3)
Balm in Gilead and Other Plays by Lanford Wilson (1208-1)
Matty and the Moron and Madonna by Herbert Lieberman (1209-X)
The Brig by Kenneth H. Brown (1210-3)
The Cavern by Jean Anouilh (1211-1)
Saved by Edward Bond (1212-X)
Eh? by Henry Livings (1213-8)
The Rimers of Eldritch and Other Plays by Lanford Wilson (1214-6)
In the Matter of J. Robert Oppenheimer by Heinar Kipphardt (1215-4)
Ergo by Jakov Lind (1216-2)
Biography: A Game by Max Frisch (1217-0)
Indians by Arthur Kopit (1218-9)
Narrow Road to the Deep North by Edward Bond (1219-7)

For a complete list of books of criticism and history of the drama, please write to Hill and Wang, 72 Fifth Avenue, New York, New York 10011.

CPSIA information can be obtained
at www.ICGtesting.com
Printed in the USA
LVHW081033050422
715333LV00010B/451